#MANAGING UP tweet Book01

140 Tips to Building an Effective Relationship with Your Boss

By Tony Deblauwe and Patrick Reilly

Foreword by S. Chris Edmonds

E-mail: info@thinkaha.com
20660 Stevens Creek Blvd., Suite 210
Cupertino, CA 95014

Published by THiNKaha®, a Happy About® imprint
20660 Stevens Creek Blvd., Suite 210, Cupertino, CA 95014
http://thinkaha.com

First Printing: July 2012
Paperback ISBN: 978-1-61699-090-9 (1-61699-090-2)
eBook ISBN: 978-1-61699-091-6 (1-61699-091-0)
Place of Publication: Silicon Valley, California, USA
Paperback Library of Congress Number: 2012934194

Trademarks

All terms mentioned in this book that are known to be trademarks or service marks have been appropriately capitalized. Neither Happy About, nor any of its imprints, can attest to the accuracy of this information. Use of a term in this book should not be regarded as affecting the validity of any trademark or service mark.

Warning and Disclaimer

Every effort has been made to make this book as complete and as accurate as possible. The information provided is on an "as is" basis. The author(s), publisher, and their agents assume no responsibility for errors or omissions. Nor do they assume liability or responsibility to any person or entity with respect to any loss or damages arising from the use of information contained herein.

Advance Praise

"The book is very practical and conveys ideas concisely in short statements (a format that resonates with old and new generations) about the relevant issue of managing up. The authors are passionate about this topic and it shows!"
Dinesh Chandra, Co-founder, DNA Global Network Inc.

"Deblauwe and Reilly have done it—a wonderful compilation of management thoughts geared toward keeping positive interaction top of mind! Anyone who manages or works with other people should read/ tweet a quote every day."
Lawrence Hall, General Manager, Network Development, Volkswagen Group of America

"*#MANAGING UP tweet* is a sweet little collection of inspired tweets. Deblauwe and Reilly have created the most efficient and delightful read I've ever experienced about how to build a healthy and productive relationship with your boss."
Robert Sutton, Professor, Stanford, Author, *Good Boss, Bad Boss*

"The need to communicate upwards is a critical ingredient of success in business. *#MANAGING UP tweet* is a great reference in the art of upward influence."
Laura Goodrich, Innovator-Speaker, On Impact Productions

"Authors Deblauwe and Reilly have hit on an effective, yet simple educational tool for managers, which 'tweets' with wisdom."
Carolyn Feuille, President & Global Coach, Esprit Global Learning

"Pearls of wisdom succinctly stated. This is a creative approach in which you are getting to the bottom line quickly as to what is important in a boss/manager relationship."
Barbara Spector, President, Smart*Moves!*

"*#MANAGING UP tweet* is a delightful compendium of quotes to help pick you up when faced with day to day challenges within an organization. Reading the quotes serve as a reminder to be wise in the workplace."
Rossella Derickson, Performance and Culture Strategist, Stanford Graduate School of Business

"This book is a handy 'hip pocket' guide for managers and employees alike and will serve as a set of time-tested reminders of new ideas and concepts."
John R. Anderson, Principal, The Glowan Consulting Group

"This book is a great tool for managers who need to effectively communicate with a modern workforce. Using the extensive experience both Tony and Patrick have gained through their years of coaching and consulting, this book delivers clear direct leadership ideas and tenets to managers striving to stay ahead in the changing world of work."
John Herb, Vice President, Human Resources, Menlo Worldwide Logistics

"These short and concise suggestions for managing up are useful at every level of every organization. Like a daily vitamin, they help you maintain a healthy working relationship with your colleagues and boss. I post a new one on my screen saver and the department bulletin board every morning, and it gives our team something to talk about. They remind us of what we often forget, and teach us new ways of working together. We look forward to each new suggestion since they are always accurate and inspiring."
Paula Grace, Director of Sales Training & Development, RingCentral

"The social media style of this book allows Tony and Patrick to hit many nails on the head in a short, punchy way. It allows you to consume a 'nibble' or a 'full meal' of great tips as you wish. No matter the consumption level you choose, you'll have plenty to think about and drive into how to improve your personal value AND your quality of life!"
Billy Wynne, VP Marketing, Con-way Freight Inc.

"The book takes complicated concepts and translates them into a simple practical thought, inspiring actions that can build the relationship between you and your manager and boost the value of you both to the organization."
Sheila Tucker, R.N., BSN, CMAS, Director of Clinical Review, Kaiser Health Plan

"Insightful, creative, and concise. *#MANAGING UP tweet* offers sound business advice without unnecessary preamble, explanation, or wasted space."
Michael B. Junge, Google Recruiter, Author, *Purple Squirrel: Stand Out, Land Interviews, and Master the Modern Job Market*

"Stop asking your boss what he can do for you! First ask what you can do for him/her and for the company. He or she will appreciate your leadership and will provide you the right environment and incentive to stay."
Gary Kowalski, Sr. VP and COO, Menlo Worldwide Logistics

"This book provides a simple tool for highlighting that good leadership and management often come down to knowing the right truths, and remembering them at the right times."
Edward Muzio, CEO, Group Harmonics, Author, *Make Work Great*

"Managing up is a critical skill everyone must learn in order to be successful at work. This book provides straightforward tips that you can apply quickly and easily to build a powerful relationship with your boss."
Anders Nancke-Krogh, CEO, MOSAIQQ

"In our working world, where there is so much information and so little time, this book and series give the 'quick fix' to sharpen our skills in a very digestible way. My clients are always looking for the pearls of wisdom they can use in their daily work life."
Joyce Reitman, Principal, EMS Partners LLC

"Tony and Patrick know relationships and people inside and out. Their book is a great read with a super concept! Enjoy!"
Dodd Starbird, Managing Partner, Implementation Partners LLC, Author, *Building Engaged Team Performance*

"I love how concise these pearls of wisdom are...just right for our fast paced lives and short attention spans!"
Amy Wallace, Sr. Account Manager, Effective Training Associates, Inc.

Acknowledgments

Many thanks to all the employees and managers without whom this book could not have been written. Your challenges on the job and drive for continuous improvement provided the impetus and insight for us to create this book. We feel fortunate to share what we learned with others to make their work life a little easier.

We also want to extend a special thanks to Dr. Laura Crawshaw and Dr. John Sullivan. Their research is a strong part of what made our work possible. And finally, big thanks and appreciation to our family, friends, and colleagues who provided their support, encouragement, and valuable time in editing our work and offering suggestions for improvement.

Tony Deblauwe and Patrick Reilly

Why We Wrote This Book

Workplaces and work cultures continue to experience rapid change amidst a globally connected and engaged business framework. How individuals and teams communicate and get work done has changed dramatically; the interpersonal connections needed to stay ahead of new challenges are more important than ever. This is especially true between bosses and employees. For employees, collaboration with one's manager forms the vital organizational layer that drives meaning and understanding about job roles, expectations, priorities, and performance. Most often, this is the place in the organization where concrete action moves forward or is held back.

We both have experienced the full spectrum of how organizational systems operate and flow. In all cases, both the content and quality of communication are vital to getting people and processes aligned and working together. Patrick has experienced this through his extensive background coaching key leaders in major companies. Tony has had a similar experience through his work in client-facing Human Resources roles where he had a bird's-eye view of how the organizational system ebbs and flows through the proper engagement of people.

Ultimately we wrote *#MANAGING UP tweet* to provide essential tips that support your efforts to build effective communication and rapport upwards, as well as to supercharge your productivity, career, and job satisfaction. We realize the significant impact a strong partnership can have and with this book our hope is to impart some valuable wisdom that can help you achieve quality relationships at work.

Tony Deblauwe (*@hr4change*)
Founder, HR4Change
http://www.hr4change.com
tony@hr4change.com

Patrick Reilly
President, Resources in Action, Inc.
http://www.resourcesinaction.com
patrick@resourcesinaction.com

How to Read a THiNKaha® Book
A Note from the Publisher

The THiNKaha series is the CliffsNotes of the 21st century. The value of these books is that they are contextual in nature. Although the actual words won't change, their meaning will change every time you read one as your context will change. Here's how to read one of these books and have it work for you.

1. Read a THiNKaha book (these slim and handy books should only take approximately 15–20 minutes of your time!) and write down one to three "aha" moments you had whilst reading it.

    a. "Aha" moments are looked at as "actionable" moments—think of a specific project you're working on, an event, a sales deal, a personal issue, etc. and see how the ahas in this book can inspire your own "aha!" moment, something that you can specifically act on.

2. Mark your calendar to re-read this book again in 30 days.

3. Repeat step #1 and write down one to three "aha" moments that grab you this time. I guarantee that they will be different than the first time.

After reading a THiNKaha book, writing down your "aha" moments, re-reading it, and writing down more "aha" moments, you'll begin to see how these books contextually apply to you. THiNKaha books advocate for continuous, life-long learning. They will help you transform your "aha" moments into actionable items with tangible results until you no longer have to say "aha!" to these moments—they'll become part of your daily practice as you continue to grow and learn.

As CEO of THiNKaha, I definitely practice what I preach. I read *#CORPORATE CULTURE tweet*, *#LEADERSHIP tweet*, and *#TEAMWORK tweet* once a month and take away two to three different action items from each of them every time. Please e-mail me your "aha" moments.

Mitchell Levy, CEO
publisher@thinkaha.com

Contents

Foreword by S. Chris Edmonds

As modern organizations grow in complexity and global reach, collaboration and communication between managers and employees are more critical than ever. Balancing individual needs and business needs requires proactive attention, nurturing, and partnership by both parties. *#MANAGING UP tweet* provides valuable insights and guidance that explains how to strategically and effectively "influence up" to enhance your most important work relationship. Use these nuggets to boost your performance, personal engagement, and job satisfaction.

S. Chris Edmonds
(@scedmonds)
Speaker, Author, Senior Consultant with the Ken Blanchard Companies

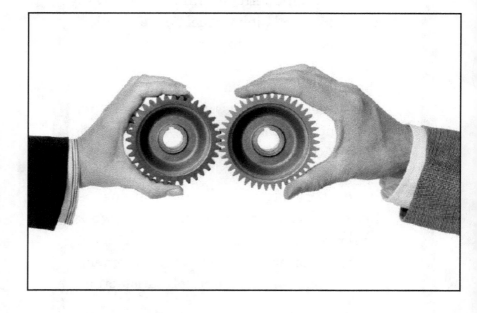

Section 1

Exploring the Boss-Employee Organizational Model

The starting point to managing up effectively is to understand the boss-employee relationship. Some people approach this relationship thinking that success is defined as being best friends. Others think it's purely a top-down hierarchical model with a "Do as I say" mentality. Neither approach or thinking represents a highly effective boss-employee dynamic. This section provides an overview of how this relationship fits into the organization and describes how you and your boss can achieve successful business outcomes.

1

Managers aren't mind readers. If you perceive a gap in communication, make sure to clearly express what you need to be successful.

2

Personal power is a great substitute for positional power; you only have it available on a limited basis. Use it wisely and strategically.

3

Any manager who does
not learn to push back and
manage up appropriately
is not adding value to
the organization.

4

Always operate with your boss to foster dignity and humility. Show your spine when it matters.

5

All managers value team members
who chop wood and carry water.
You truly get to know people
by doing work with them.

6

Your personal power gains momentum
from your attitude and work quality,
not the title on your business card.

7

Bosses and employees achieve success through mutually beneficial outcomes that encompass both business and individual objectives.

8

Employees are an asset to the organization just like managers; managers are just higher up the food chain.

9

When you don't speak up to your boss when something bothers you, the perception is that the concern is not that important to you.

10

Establish your value in the work hierarchy by leveraging your knowledge and experience on critical issues.

11

Managers coach, mentor, and lead their employees through change in order to satisfy strategic challenges.

12

Support your boss—be flexible,
resourceful, insightful, and impactful.

13

Stress and pressure are constants
to getting work done, so include
some levity when appropriate
to boost the mood.

14

A key indicator for employee job fulfillment and satisfaction is the leadership skills of their managers.[1]

---

1. Michael Leimbach, Ph.D., "Redefining Employee Satisfaction: Business Performance, Employee Fulfillment, and Leadership Practices" (research report), *Wilson Learning*, 2006, **http://bit.ly/wilsonlearning**.

15

Mutual recognition and appreciation for value-added contributions focus bosses and employees on the things that matter.

16

Good managers know the difference when employees say things out of passion versus negativity.

17

On any given issue ask yourself, "Does it really matter?" to avoid turning minor concerns into major ones with your boss.

18

Always conduct yourself
ethically and assume the best
from those with whom you work.

19

Listen and test. If your boss
is using "you" and "I" you have one
kind of relationship. If you hear
"we," you have another.

20

The best working relationship is when employees operate to their strengths and managers work to encourage and enhance those strengths.

21

If you ask your boss about your performance or future potential, be prepared that the feedback may not match what you think of yourself.

22

Doing your job and being personally accountable for results must remain your top priority, regardless of any issues you have with your boss.

23

Don't let where you think you fall in the hierarchy affect pitching an innovative idea to your boss.

24

Good managers actively seek to ensure their people don't fail and provide them opportunities for growth.

25

First and foremost, employees and managers are measured and paid on the quality of their work, not their personalities.

26

A strong work ethic, intelligence, results, and quality of interaction usually create a good impression with people.

27

Don't ask your manager for personal favors that potentially risk confusing the nature of the relationship.

28

Don't question the business judgment of your boss on certain issues. ("Does it really matter that we get this done by Friday afternoon?")

29

Don't make idle threats ("If you don't, I'll quit!"). Ultimatums are forbidden regardless of the circumstances.

30

Don't bring your boss into conversations that involve conflict with others. Don't say things like, "I think Bob is out to get me."

31

Managers are like good referees— they are often asked to make quick, sometimes unpopular, decisions without context or explanation.

32

Congenial relationships between supervisors and employees lead to higher retention and productivity.[2]

2. Ian T. Brown, "In Western Europe, More Partners Than Bosses," *GALLUP World*, January 30, 2009, http://bit.ly/partners-bosses.

33

Positive impacts on key business metrics correlate directly with increased employee engagement.[3]

---

3. GALLUP, "Employee Engagement," *GALLUP*, accessed May 2012, http://bit.ly/LKCqAJ.

34

Don't lie to make up excuses for a day off. Speak the truth even if it makes you uncomfortable.

35

Bosses and employees exist to partner and effectively meet organizational commitments.

Section II

Communicating the Rules of Engagement

This section focuses on the framework of effective communication. These tips describe how you and your boss can set the appropriate tone by being aligned on role clarity and performance expectations.

36

Let your boss know

what you say "yes" to

and what you say "no" to;

these are your core values.

37

Clarify and negotiate the key aspects of your role and the outcomes your boss expects from you.

38

Learn when and how to escalate issues to your boss early and use facts, not emotions or speculation.

39

Select the right people when building your team. Then do what is needed to get them to perform as one.

40

Every boss has something that is most important. Find out what it is and place it on or near the top of your "to-do" list.

41

Misunderstanding and
miscommunication of goals,
roles, and expectations
are the most common
roadblocks between
employees and managers.

42

Some bosses are readers, some are talkers. Learn which one your boss is and initiate interaction through the preferred mode.

43

Everyone has various bottom lines about quality of interaction, timeliness, etc. Learn your boss's bottom line and never sink below it.

44

Be accountable for your actions
and let your boss know early
if there are problems.

45

Get to know your boss's
style and engage with it.

46

More employees are satisfied with their work when they see their supervisor as a partner.[4]

4. Ian T. Brown, "In Western Europe, More Partners Than Bosses," *GALLUP World*, January 30, 2009, http://bit.ly/partners-bosses.

47

Leading employee demotivators: failure to state real issues, futurism,[5] and asking for input despite decisions already made.[6]

5. Futurism: "always looking down the road at distant goals or a vision, and not being present." Ray B. Williams, "How to Demotivate Workers," *Wired for Success* (*Psychology Today* blog), October 30, 2011, http://bit.ly/how-demotivate-workers.
6. Ibid.

48

Try not to give your boss anything
to fret about over the weekend.

49

If your boss is a bully, become the one
who knows how to limit his charge.

50

Convey information and issues to your boss in a methodical way and avoid overwhelming him or her.

51

51% of actively disengaged employees would get rid of their manager if they could.[7]

---

7. Bryant Ott and Emily Killham, "Would You Fire Your Boss?," *GALLUP Management Journal*, September 13, 2007, http://gmj.gallup.com/content/28597/would-fire-your-boss.aspx.

52

Don't randomly voice your opinions about others without the facts and data to verify.

53

Schedule regular check-ins with your boss for important updates and to discuss your top challenges.

54

Enhance your utility in your boss's eyes by making your individual style, views, and goals clear; then deliver when given the chance.

55

Close the gap of communication with your boss by closing the gap of physical distance—meet your boss face-to-face.

56

Don't rely primarily on digital communication methods (email, IM, etc.) to make decisions if there is a disagreement on how to proceed.

57

Display your effort every day in your thinking and always volunteer to do more without being asked.

58

If you need to go
to your boss's boss
about an issue, think
about what you want; don't
necessarily expect action.

59

Look to your boss as
a good barometer of
what's happening in the
organization & how broader
changes could impact you
and your job function.

60

Managers can balance employees' need for growth by positioning them in ways that stretch, not discourage, their abilities.

61

Tradeoffs on a project are best viewed as a two-way dialogue of what ideas stay or go, not a contest of will or ego.

62

If your manager is inattentive when you are speaking, try varying your delivery, using a different approach, or changing the subject.

63

Find the right time to approach your boss about certain trying subjects. What is top of mind for you may not be top of mind for him or her.

64

If necessary, challenge your boss on a key decision if the business stakes are high & his/her wrong move could result in damaging outcomes.

65

If you introduce everything in context you can get people to see it differently. This is known as priming.

66

What do you need to make visible so your boss gets it? Many times what is real and what is needed to move forward are under the surface.

67

Many organizations' value
resides in intangibles;
high quality employee
relationships are a key factor
in providing value.[8]

8. Ocean Tomo, "Ocean Tomo 300 Patent Index," *Ocean Tomo*,
accessed May 2012, http://bit.ly/eWT7qc.

68

65% of employees aren't inspired by their supervisors.[9]

9. Chad Brooks, "Bosses Aren't Doing Enough to Inspire
   Employees, Research Finds," *BusinessNewsDaily* (blog),
   December 12, 2011 (9:25 a.m.),
   http://bit.ly/BossesInspringEmployees.

69

Partnering with your manager means asking the right questions, doing the right things in the right way and at the right time.

Section III: Building a Foundation of Mutual Respect

Section III

Building a Foundation of Mutual Respect

Once a communication framework is in place as a foundation to the relationship, the next step is to build a partnership that draws upon the strengths of both boss and employee competencies, knowledge, and contribution.

70

Don't ever put your boss
on the spot in front of his/her
boss or other higher-ups without
good and timely information.

71

A team member should feel like
the most important person to you
at the moment. Stop what you are
doing and make eye contact.

72

Pay as much attention to *how* your boss likes things done as well as *what* she or he wants and needs done.

73

Treat everyone on the team equally. Favoritism erodes a manager's credibility and weakens your team.

74

The full respect test:
When you meet, do you
have their full attention
or are they speaking with
others, answering mail,
checking messages?

75

When you feel good about the relationship with your boss, you project a positive energy that enhances both your team and work culture.

76

Make sure your communication in writing is clear and concise and ensure that you speak up in meetings at the right time.

77

The most important motivator for employees is knowing that they are making progress.[10]

10. Teresa Amabile and Steven Kramer, "How to completely, utterly destroy an employee's work life," *On Leadership* (*The Washington Post* blog), March 6, 2012, http://wapo.st/on-leadership.

78

Remember, everything you do is judged. Act and dress accordingly.

79

Think about how you can position information so that your boss can see the issue through the right lens.

80

It is always easy to focus on what's *not* working. How can you help your boss see what is needed to help move things forward?

81

Some leadership attention is gained by regularly and consistently being silent and then speaking up at the right moment.

82

What are the key assets you need
to activate to influence your boss?
What have you not thought of yet?

83

Employees can support their
bosses by targeting priorities,
being resourceful, and improvising
in the face of crisis.

84

When coaching employees, always speak to company expectations—this helps reinforce standards of performance and conduct.

85

Be a problem solver, not a problem starter.

86

Find a way to state your POV without hyperbole or an emphatic "no."

87

Rumors come from the thinnest of details and can be detrimental to productivity so don't encourage them!

88

Strive to help each other improve ways of working so you benefit both as individuals and as a team.

89

Always maintain a strong excellence orientation so that you are regarded as indispensable.

90

View criticism from your boss as an opportunity for further discussion and reserve judgment on his or her motivations for the feedback.

91

Like you do for everybody else, give your boss the benefit of the doubt.

92

Be accountable for all that
you do and say.

93

Changing the relationship
with your boss involves objectively
addressing issues and business
requirements appropriately.

94

Emotions can get the best of you when trying to get your boss to see your point of view...step back if you have to.

95

Don't spend too much energy trying to predict what your boss will say or do as it only robs you of power and mental focus.

96

A quality pair of hands
is always valued.

97

Present your ideas and thinking
on a subject with the data to back
up your proposal.

98

Managers show respect to employees when they listen actively rather than disagree vehemently.

99

In formal presentations to senior management, make your boss look good and never generate unwanted surprises.

100

When you are upset, before expressing your concerns, determine what being respectful looks like.

101

Celebrating, not condemning, personality quirks can act as a catalyst to fresh thinking and perspectives.

102

Managers who become better coaches get higher employee productivity, engagement, and financial performance.[11]

---

11. "Leaders who coach, develop employees see 3 times greater impact," *J. J. Keller & Associates*, November 10, 2011, http://bit.ly/jjkeller.

103

"Disengaged" employees cost the American economy $350B/year.[12] One of the biggest factors in engagement: relationship with direct manager.

12. Barb Sanford, "The High Cost of Disengaged Employees," *GALLUP Management Journal*, April 15, 2002, http://bit.ly/DisengagedEmployees.

104

55% say their manager influences their productivity.[13]

---

13. Mark Eggleton, "Rewards bring out the best in workers, says SHL boss," *The Australian*, June 25, 2011 (12:00 a.m.), http://bit.ly/rewards-bring-out-the-best.

105

When you feel good about the relationship with your boss you project a positive energy that enhances both team and work culture.[14]

14. Tony Schwartz, "Why Appreciation Matters So Much," *Harvard Business Review* (blog), January 23, 2012 (9:44 a.m.), http://bit.ly/why-appreciation-matters.

106

Lack of rapport with your boss predicts the risk for depression and other psychiatric problems in the workplace.[15]

---

15. Willow Lawson, "Good Boss, Bad Boss," *Psychology Today*, November 1, 2005, last reviewed December 28, 2011, http://bit.ly/good-boss-bad-boss.

107

Don't rush to find the perfect
interaction with your boss;
give it time to mature until
you can both approach it
honestly and transparently.

108

Employees want to work with good managers who ensure their people don't fail and provide them with opportunities for growth.

Section IV

Achieving Perfect Alignment with Your Boss

Negotiation is vital to a healthy boss-employee relationship because it ensures that communication channels are fluid and humming. The appropriate levels of "give and take" extend benefits beyond the immediate relationship and are felt by others in the organization.

109

Influence is about presenting your ideas in a way that aligns with your boss's needs and expectations.

110

Check for understanding on agreed-upon next steps and verbally summarize the actions to be taken (and, if need be, in writing).

111

Demonstrate leadership with your team: clarify vision, align resources, and develop coalitions with other teams to get work done.

112

Be willing to reinvent yourself, your role, and your approach to meet changing business conditions and show your resourcefulness.

113

Managers create stakeholders
when they regularly involve their
employees in sharing information
and making big decisions.

114

Give your boss the executive summary
slide and have the next 100 on backup.

115

Don't think in terms of "want/need" when you talk to your boss; think about his/her position and then structure your message accordingly.

116

If you encounter roadblocks when trying to achieve your goals, revise the process steps, not the goals.

117

Countries in which employees feel their supervisors treat them well tend to have higher GDP per capita.[16]

16. Ian T. Brown, "In Western Europe, More Partners Than Bosses," *GALLUP World*, January 30, 2009, http://bit.ly/western-europe-partners-bosses.

118

Don't ask your boss to make your decisions about process, people, or technology, but do ask for an opinion.

119

Negotiation is not about who has the power, it's about establishing mutual interests and developing sustainable solutions.

120

When dealing with gray areas be specific about the issue you're trying to address and the input you're seeking.

121

Confidence (without arrogance) towards your boss builds both credibility and trust.

122

Acknowledge your boss's efforts regularly to those who need to know.

123

Often innovative solutions require employees and bosses to look beyond policies and procedures and to be creative together.

124

Managers make tough business decisions that negatively impact others but that doesn't necessarily mean they are insensitive or incompetent.

125

Be the one on a boss's team who engenders collaboration and communication, not the one who makes the noise that requires firefighting.

126

Keep your knowledge base updated and boost your relevancy to your manager by regularly checking, analyzing, and sharing external trends.

127

You may not always know your boss's intent in responding to your issues, so always give him or her the benefit of the doubt.

128

Don't get bogged down in who gets credit for accomplishments; a good working relationship assumes recognition is properly attributed.

129

Who are the organizational cheerleaders who will support and advocate on behalf of your and your boss's initiatives? Connect with them.

130

Encourage your boss to hold all-hands meetings to share info about the status and strategies of the organization and how it is performing.

131

70% of corporate leaders are highly concerned about retaining critical talent.[17]

---

17. Deloitte, "Blueprints for the new normal," *Talent Edge 2020* (December 2010), http://bit.ly/kSB4jb.

132

The easiest way to test if your boss hates you is to check with other team members.[18]

---

18. Paul Hellman, "What to Do When Your Boss Hates You," *CNBC.com* (blog), February 2, 2012 (9:21 a.m.), http://www.cnbc.com/id/46235789.

133

Highly engaged employees get 26% higher revenue & 13% higher shareholder return; a strong boss relationship is a key factor.[19]

19. Watson Wyatt Worldwide, "Driving Business Results Through Continuous Engagement" (WorkUSA Survey Report), 2008/2009, http://bit.ly/researchpdf.

134

Command and control is for TV remotes, not for getting people to respond by doing their jobs differently.

135

Say thank you in an authentic way when your boss cuts you slack due to extenuating circumstances.

136

Show your humility by continuing a dialogue with your boss even if your ideas do not get represented.

137

Although a failure to execute goals stings, if positioned properly, it can be the springboard to better ideas and focus.

138

Innovation embraces failure to find the diamond in the rough. The same is true with building the right communication style upwards.

139

If it's true that you see what you want to see then imagine your boss as a crusader for excellence—for you, the team, and the business.

140

"Coming together is a beginning. Keeping together is progress. Working together is success."

- Henry Ford[20]

20. Henry Ford (1863–1947): American industrialist and founder of the Ford Motor Company.

About the Authors

Tony Deblauwe is the founder of consulting firm HR4Change. For fifteen years Tony has worked in Silicon Valley high-tech companies managing a variety of Human Resources functions. He is an award-winning author, app developer, and blogger. He has been quoted in a variety of media sources, including TheLadders, CareerBuilder, Monster.com, and CBS MoneyWatch.

Patrick Reilly is President of Resources in Action, Inc., a firm specializing in executive coaching and consulting. He has worked extensively with leaders in the health care, financial services, technology, and utility sectors for more than twenty-five years, both internationally and in the US. His passion is getting leaders into action for success and satisfaction. Patrick works primarily with leaders in transition and senior leadership teams. He is an expert in dealing with challenges related to leaders with an abrasive style.

Books in the THiNKaha® Series

The THiNKaha book series is for thinking adults who lack the time or desire to read long books, but want to improve themselves with knowledge of the most up-to-date subjects. THiNKaha is a leader in timely, cutting-edge books and mobile applications from relevant experts that provide valuable information in a fun, Twitter-brief format for a fast-paced world.

They are available online at **http://thinkaha.com** or at other online and physical bookstores.

THiNKaha® Learning/Training Programs Designed to Take You to the Next Level NOW!

THiNKaha delivers high-quality, cost-effective continuous learning in easy-to-understand, worthwhile, and digestible chunks. Fifteen minutes with a THiNKaha book will allow readers to have one or more "aha" moments. Spending less than two hours a month with a THiNKaha Learning Program (either online or in person) will provide learners with an opportunity to truly digest the topic at hand and connect with gurus whose subject-matter expertise gives them an actionable roadmap to enhance their skills.

Offered online, on demand, and/or in person, these engaging programs feature gurus (ours and yours) on such relevant topics as Leadership, Management, Sales, Marketing, Work-Life Balance, Project Management, Social Media and Networking, Presentation Skills, and other topics of your choosing. The "learning" audience, whether it is clients, employees, or partners, can now experience high-quality learning that will enhance your brand value and empower your company as a thought leader. This program fits a real need where time and the high cost of developing custom content are no longer an option for every organization.

> *"This program has been very successful and in demand within Cisco. The vision and implementation of the THiNKaha Learning Program has enabled us to offer high-quality content both live and on-demand. Their gurus and experts are knowledgeable and very engaging."*
>
> **- Bette Daoust, Ph.D**
> **Former Learning and Development Manager, Cisco, and Internal Program Manager for THiNKaha Guru Series**

Visit THiNKaha Learning Program at http://thinkaha.com/learning.

Just **THiNK**...

- **C**ontinuous Employee/Client/Prospect Learning
- **O**ngoing Thought Leadership Development
- **N**otable Experts Presenting on Relevant Topics
- **T**ime Your Attendees Can Afford – 15 min. to 2 hrs/mo.
- **I**nformation Delivered in Digestible Chunks
- **N**ame the Topic—We Help You Provide Expert Best Practices
- **U**nderstand and Implement the Takeaways
- **I**nternal Expertise Shared Externally
- **T**raining/Prospecting Cost Decreases, Effectiveness Increases
- **Y**ou Win, They Win!

www.ingramcontent.com/pod-product-compliance
Lightning Source LLC
Chambersburg PA
CBHW071223050326
40689CB00011B/2435